ENIGMAS *of* HISTORY

THE MYSTERIES OF STONEHENGE

WORLD
BOOK

a Scott Fetzer company
Chicago
www.worldbook.com

World Book edition of "Enigmas de la historia" by Editorial Sol 90.

Enigmas de la historia
El complejo de Stonehenge

This edition licensed from Editorial Sol 90 S.L.
Copyright 2013 Editorial Sol S.L. All rights reserved.

English-language revised edition copyright 2014, 2016
World Book, Inc.
Enigmas of History
The Mysteries of Stonehenge

World Book, Inc.
180 North LaSalle Street
Suite 900
Chicago, Illinois 60601
USA

For information about other World Book publications, visit our
website at **www.worldbook.com** or call **1-800-967-5325.**

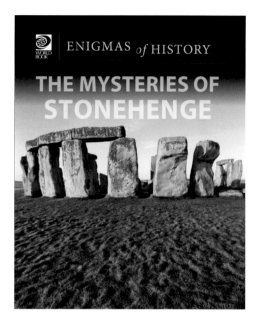

People began building at Stonehenge—a prehistoric
site of huge, rough-cut stones set in a circle—in
about 3000 B.C. Building on the site took place for
the next 1,500 years. Archaeological excavations in
the area revealed that Stonehenge was part of a
larger ceremonial center.

© Steve Vidler, Alamy Images

Library of Congress Cataloging-in-Publication Data

Complejo de Stonehenge. English
   The mysteries of Stonehenge. -- English-language revised edition
      pages cm. -- (Enigmas of history)
   Includes index.
   Orignially published as: El complejo de Stonehenge, by Editorial Sol S.L.,
c2013.
   Summary: "An exploration of the questions and mysteries that have puzzled
scholars and experts about the Neolithic site of Stonehenge. Features include
a map, fact boxes, biographies of famous experts on Stonehenge, places to see
and visit, a glossary, further readings, and index"-- Provided by publisher.
   ISBN 978-0-7166-2667-1
   1. Stonehenge (England)--Juvenile literature. 2. Wiltshire (England)--
Antiquities--Juvenile literature. 3. Megalithic monuments--England--
Wiltshire--Juvenile literature. I. World Book, Inc. II. Title.
DA142.C6613 2014
936.2'319--dc23
                          2014008214

Set ISBN: 978-0-7166-2660-2

Printed in China by Shenzhen Wing King Tong Paper
Products Co., Ltd., Shenzhen, Guangdong
3rd printing March 2018

Staff

Executive Committee

President
Jim O'Rourke

Vice President and Editor in Chief
Paul A. Kobasa

Vice President, Finance
Donald D. Keller

Vice President, Marketing
Jean Lin

Director, Human Resources
Bev Ecker

Editorial

Managing Editor,
Annuals and Topical Reference
Christine Sullivan

Editors
Jake Bumgardner
Lynn Durbin
Nicholas Kilzer

Manager, Indexing Services
David Pofelski

Administrative Assistant
Ethel Matthews

Manager, Contracts & Compliance
(Rights & Permissions)
Loranne K. Shields

Senior Manager, Publishing
Operations
Timothy Falk

Manufacturing/Production

Manufacturing Manager
Sandra Johnson

Production/Technology
Manager
Anne Fritzinger

Proofreader
Nathalie Strassheim

Graphics and Design

Senior Art Director
Tom Evans

Senior Designer
Don Di Sante

Media Researcher
Rosalia Bledsoe

Manager, Cartographic Services
Wayne K. Pichler

Senior Cartographer
John M. Rejba

Glossary There is a glossary of terms on page 44. Terms defined in the glossary are in boldface **(type that looks like this)** on their first appearance on any *spread* (two facing pages). Words that are difficult to say are followed by a pronunciation (pruh NUHN see AY shuhn) the first time they are mentioned.

Contents

The Mystery and Majesty of Stonehenge

Stonehenge—a great circle of stones in England—is one of the greatest mysteries of the ancient world. Since some 400 years ago, when dealers in ancient objects claimed that Stonehenge had been a pagan temple, theories about the site have multiplied. An astronomical computer, a mathematical calendar, a focus of energies that some believe Earth possesses, and a healing center—these are just some of the ideas about Stonehenge raised in recent years. Which of these ideas are possible, and which are flights of fancy?

This monumental complex was built by a society in the **Stone Age.** The Stone Age is the period before humans used tools made of metal. It began about 2.5 million years ago, but the date at which it ended varies with place. In England, the Stone Age ended about 4,500 years ago.

How did ancient people with such primitive tools build such a sophisticated structure? The blocks of **sandstone**—called **sarsen**—that were used in Stonehenge weigh up to 38.5 tons (35 metric tons). They were transported 19 miles (30.5 kilometers) to the site. (Sandstone is a type of rock composed chiefly of sand that has been "cemented" by pressure or by minerals.) The inner ring of **bluestones** (blocks of blueish volcanic stone) weigh between 4.4 and 9 tons (4 and 8 metric tons). Scientists recently discovered from their composition that they came from a nearby outcropping, about 1.8 miles (3 kilometers) away from the site originally proposed as their source nearly a century ago.

Thanks to modern **archaeology,** we know something about the era in which Stonehenge was built. Experts have agreed on a general time frame. Construction began between 3000 and 2920 B.C. (Phase 1), with a circular enclosure and a circle of small pits. Known as "Aubrey Holes," they possibly once contained bluestones. After the Aubrey Holes were in place, the builders of Stonehenge erected wooden posts. At some point, in the period from 2620 to 2480 B.C. (Phase 2), the bluestones were placed in a circle around the horseshoe, a formation of five **trilithons** (TRY luh thonz—two stones standing upright with a stone across the top). This was enclosed within a circle of 30 blocks of sarsen. It is believed that around these dates, other stones were also erected in the entrance area. The *axis* (central line) of Stonehenge aligns with the setting sun on the winter **solstice** and with the rising sun on the summer solstice in the Northern Hemisphere.

Three additional stages of construction have been identified. During Phase 3 (2480 to 2280 B.C.), a new circle of bluestones was raised in the center of Stonehenge, built with stones from Bluehenge (see page 21), which was located next to the River Avon before it was taken down. During this period Stonehenge and Bluehenge were connected by a road known as "The Avenue." During Phase 4 (2270 to 2020 B.C.), the bluestones were redistributed, and during Phase 5 (2020 to 1520 B.C.), some were sculpted.

In recent years, new excavations have helped us to understand Stonehenge in *context* (background)—and in archaeology, context is everything—with the discovery of a settlement buried underneath the great Durrington Walls enclosure, just 2 miles (3.2 kilometers) away. Together with Bluehenge, Durrington Walls demonstrates that Stonehenge was not an isolated site but was part of a larger complex of stones and wooden circles, with the two centers connected by the River Avon. While Stonehenge was likely the domain of the dead, the wooden circles of Durrington Walls were the place where the living celebrated the solstices.

In 2008, archaeologists excavated part of "The Avenue" that leads from Stonehenge along the axis of the solstice. They found that its ridges and trenches follow a series of natural hills that are aligned with the solstice. The prehistoric people observed this alignment in the natural landscape and later built upon it with ridges and trenches.

Stonehenge: Neolithic Remains

Visited by thousands of people every year, this **megalith** (structure made of large stones by **prehistoric** people) was thought by some scientists to be an *astronomical observatory* (a place from which to view the stars and planets), and by others to be a temple for worshiping the dead. The mystery remains.

The **Stone Age** is divided into three periods—Paleolithic, Mesolithic, and **Neolithic.** The most recent period is the Neolithic—marked by the beginning of agriculture and the use of polished stone weapons and tools.

In the Neolithic Period, western Europe, and especially England, was filled with simple constructions called **cromlechs.** Cromlechs were stone circles made up of a series of **menhirs** (large vertical stones) placed into circles or ovals. Among the more than 1,000 cromlechs in the United Kingdom and Ireland today, the best known are Callanish and Brodgar in Scotland; and Castlerigg, Long Meg, Avebury, and Stonehenge in England.

Though similar in some ways, important differences exist between these structures. Avebury, near to Stonehenge, is so large—1,099 feet (335 meters) in diameter— that it is hard to see its circular shape from the ground. Callanish, whose biggest stones are 16 feet (4.8 meters) tall, only measures 42 feet (12.8 meters) in diameter.

The most extraordinary of all the prehistoric monuments in England is, without a doubt, Stonehenge. It is located in the south of England, some 86 miles (138.5 kilometers) west of London. Stonehenge does not stand out because of its size—the outer circle only measures 98 feet (30 meters) in diameter. It is the complexity of Stonehenge and its role as part of an extensive grouping of ancient ruins that make the site outstanding.

As a matter of fact, the complexity of Stonehenge led **archaeologists** to distinguish between cromlechs—simple circles of stones—and what they came to call **henges,** a name taken from Stonehenge itself. The word *henge* designates a stone- or wood-circle complex of prehistoric origin made up of a circular *embankment* (a raised bank of earth or stones) with smaller circular areas in the middle. The center areas may contain gravestones or structures of stone or wood.

A map or aerial photo of the area allows us to see that Stonehenge includes large menhirs, a trench, an embankment, a circle of small holes, various gravestones, isolated **monoliths** (a column made of a single large stone), and many other ancient remains in its surroundings.

MILESTONE
Stonehenge is a masterpiece of engineering. The 30 giant stones that formed the outer circle—17 of which still remain in place—weigh some 55 tons (50 metric tons) each.

A FEAT OF CONSTRUCTION

In an area of 2.5 acres (10,000 square meters)—the equivalent of a soccer field—the great diversity of **Neolithic** remains is not the most impressive thing about Stonehenge, nor does it explain what has made this monument one of the world's most visited **prehistoric** sites. A comparison of Stonehenge with any of the other stone circles discussed earlier shows why Stonehenge is so special. The other circles of the United Kingdom and continental Europe are formed of unpolished **monoliths,** raised as they were found. The **menhirs** of Stonehenge, however, were polished to give them an oblong shape with flat sides that allowed them to hold up a third **megalith** as a **lintel** (a horizontal stone placed on top of two stone columns). This change put the builders of Stonehenge on a much higher technological level than the creators of Callanish, Brodgar, or Castlerigg.

To fairly evaluate the feats of the Stonehenge builders, scholars must place the work in the context of its location and time period. In any era, the evolution of the historic periods presents notable differences depending on place. For example, around 3000 B.C.—the beginning phase of building at Stonehenge—the cultures of *Mesopotamia* (the area

that is now Iraq, eastern Syria, and southeastern Turkey) had already entered the **Bronze Age.** The people of the European Atlantic, however, were still in the **Stone Age.** The Sumerians of Uruk, in Mesopotamia, invented the wheel and introduced writing between 3500 and 3300 B.C. In the coming centuries, the builders at Stonehenge would have found moving the monoliths much easier with the help of wheels. But these things took additional centuries to arrive in Britain.

The difference in the level of cultural advancement between the Near East and

Europe is evident when one considers that the initial circles of Stonehenge were erected at approximately the same time as the very advanced Great Pyramid of Giza in Egypt.

The monuments of one of the greatest civilizations of history should not, however, take away from the construction feats of the population of southwest Britain at the same time. Especially considering that the stones used at Stonehenge were not native to the area and that those stones were carved with an exactitude more usual for a carpenter than a stonecutter.

None of the types of stone found in Stonehenge are from the area. The blocks of **bluestone,** which are up to 6.5 feet (2 meters) high and weigh 4.4 tons (4 metric tons), come from mountains 150 miles (241.4 kilometers) away. The monoliths of *silica* (a common mineral) **sandstone,** some of which are over 23 feet (7 meters) tall and weigh 44 tons (40 metric tons), were moved from a site 18 miles (29 kilometers) away.

Stonehenge was built over a long period of time. According to the most recent studies, the building began some 5,000 years ago. Around 3000 B.C., the people of the plains in the

southwest of England built
an **embankment** and a circular ditch that was 378 feet
(115 meters) in diameter.
They then dug 56 holes
within that circle—known
as the "Aubrey Holes." They
are named for John Aubrey,
an early British **archaeologist** from the 1600's. The
Aubrey Holes may once
have held the bluestones.

In the centuries following
3000 B.C., this circular area
with two entrances seems to
have been filled with more
complex wooden structures.
These possibly were related
to funeral ceremonies that
were practiced in the area.
Four to five centuries later,

around 2600 or 2500 B.C.,
the builders of Stonehenge
raised the sandstone monoliths and changed the positions of the bluestones.

THE AVENUE
Inside the circles of bluestones and **sarsen** stones is a
final structure, this time in
the shape of a horseshoe. It
is made up of five sandstone
trilithons; it is open toward
the northeast; and it is
flanked by an internal line
of smaller bluestones facing
in the same direction—
toward the daybreak of the
summer solstice. Between
2480 and 2280 B.C., an avenue 2 miles (3.2 kilometers)

long was built. It reached
the River Avon and formed
part of the grouping of prehistoric remains found
around Stonehenge. These
nearby remains include the
Cursus (a wide, almost
straight road 2 miles long),
the Woodhenge Circles
(similar to Stonehenge but
made of wood), and
Durrington Walls. The latter is an enormous circle of
houses around which were
found remains from a
Neolithic population.

The discovery of
Woodhenge, at the begin-
ning of the 1900's, was
important to the **archaeological** research exploring

the evolution of Stonehenge. The remains of the woodwork indicate that, before erecting the stone structure, the builders had built a base of tree trunks that remained in place for several centuries. This explains why, when they decided to substitute stone for wood, they treated the stone as if they were carpenters. Instead of joining the stones with mortar, or stacking them like a dry stone wall, the Stonehenge builders used dovetail joints—a technique carpenters call "mortise and tenon"—which has held the monoliths together with precision, strength, and reliability. That half of the structure has remained standing for 4,500 years, in an extremely windy, humid, and cold area, demonstrates the great ability of the carpenters who worked the stone.

The location of Stonehenge allows the monument to be seen from a distance of 1.25 miles (2.1 kilometers) from almost all angles. Its alignment with the rising sun in the summer **solstice** and with the sunset in the winter solstice fed the theory for many years that it was an astronomical observatory and a place for worshiping gods associated with natural astronomy.

As a matter of fact, the neighboring circles of Woodhenge and Durrington Walls also have alignments that coincide with the solstices. Research by archaeologists suggests, however, that the original purpose of Stonehenge was not related to astronomy but rather to the worship of the dead, though no doubt the builders knew much about the pathways of the sun through the sky and used them as reference points for building the monument.

Gerald Hawkins
(1928-2003)

British astronomer Gerald Hawkins became famous when he published a study about Stonehenge in which he claimed the Neolithic construction was an **astronomical calendar.** With wooden posts or stone columns positioned in the correct places in a circle, the sun would mark the day of an important astronomical event by shining through a certain opening or gate. His work, *Stonehenge Decoded,* was published by the magazine *Nature* in 1963. An edited version appeared in a book of the same name two years later. Hawkins carried out his work by entering the positions of the great stones and other characteristics of Stonehenge into a very early IBM computer and using the data obtained to model the movements of the sun and moon. Thanks to this study, Hawkins is today considered one of the fathers of *archeoastronomy* (the scientific study of how ancient people understood the sky, the stars, the planets, and how that knowledge was used in their culture).

THEORY With a doctorate in **radioastronomy** (astronomy that studies the radio frequencies of objects in the sky), Hawkins claimed Stonehenge was a **"Neolithic** computer" which, among other things, served to predict **eclipses.**

NEOLITHIC The contributions of Piggott to archaeology were linked with this prehistoric age.

Stuart Piggott
(1910-1996)

British professor Stuart Piggott was a specialist in **Celtic** culture who actively participated in the excavations at Stonehenge done in the middle of the last century. This venture led to the discovery of engravings made with hatchets, clubs, and daggers on the **sarsen** stones in the areas around Stonehenge.

M. Parker Pearson (1957-)

British archaeologist M. Parker Pearson, working first for the University of Sheffield and now for the University College London, dedicated years of his career to Stonehenge. With his team, he discovered the site called "Bluehenge" (or "Bluestonehenge"), named for the color of the 27 stones placed in the area. Mike Parker Pearson was part of the Stonehenge Riverside Project, financed by the National Geographic Society and the United Kingdom's Arts and Humanities Research Council, with the support of the English Heritage. During this project, it was discovered that the area where the **megalithic** structure stands functioned as a cemetery for more than 500 years. Members of an ancient ruling clan and their descendants were buried there. It also highlighted the significance of the River Avon, which "formed a channel between the living and the dead . . . . people left the land of the living at the river and entered the land of the dead in Stonehenge."

CONNECTION According to Parker Pearson, Durrington Walls represents the land of the living and Stonehenge the domain of their dead ancestors. The two sites were linked by seasonal **processions** that followed a trajectory indicated by the paths and the river.

"I don't believe that ordinary people were buried at Stonehenge. It was a special place in that period. Anyone buried there must have had good credentials." M. P. P.

Richard C. Atkinson
(1920-1994)

British archaeologist Richard C. Atkinson worked in close collaboration with Stuart Piggott and formed his own theory about the construction of Stonehenge. He directed a series of excavations in the area between 1950 and 1964. Unfortunately he did not keep a suitable record of this work, and his discoveries remained unknown for years. After Atkinson's death, some archaeological pieces obtained in his excavations and more than 2,000 photographs taken in the area were found in his home.

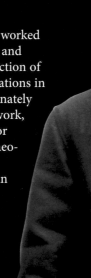

CALCULATION According to Professor Atkinson, the transportation of each stone that forms part of Stonehenge required the efforts of 1,500 men and took at least 7 weeks.

Early Astronomers?

The Stonehenge complex is a masterpiece made by an ancient society interested in the observation of the stars. The people of Stonehenge had begun a difficult shift from the traditional life of hunting to the hard labor of agricultural life.

The Astronomical Calendar

Some **archaeologists** believe that Stonehenge was a temple for the observation of astronomical events, a calendar that permitted farmers to anticipate the start of the seasons and to guide their activities.

THE STRUCTURE

Stonehenge is made up of **concentric circles** (differently sized circles centered on one point) of **megaliths** of up to 16 feet (4.8 meters) high. Perfectly placed in the ground, they can calculate the movement of the sun and the moon and indicate the **solstices** and **eclipses.**

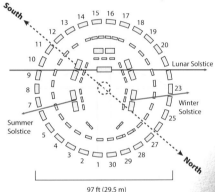

97 ft (29.5 m)

SOLSTICES

Times in the year during which the sun reaches its highest point in the tropics. The summer solstice is the longest day of the year, the winter solstice the shortest.

From the Neolithic to the Bronze Age

Every 18.6 years the moon reaches an extreme azimuth at Stonehenge—that is, the moon lines up over the sun when seen from this spot.

----- Path of the sun
----- Path of the moon

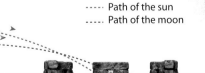

THE OUTER STONES

They are known as **sarsens**. The **lintels** weigh up to 7.7 tons (7 metric tons) and the pillars 27.5 tons (25 metric tons).

SECOND RING

THIRD RING

Slaughter Stone

Did Any Other Culture Help the Ancient Britons in the Construction of Stonehenge?

During one of the archaeological excavations carried out in the area where Stonehenge was built, the team headed by English professor Richard Atkinson found a dagger made of stone whose carved edge was very similar to the daggers from the Greek civilization that flourished in Mycenae (my SEE nee) in 1500 B.C. That discovery caused them to speculate if the Mycenaeans may have been involved in the construction of the monument. Later scholars decided this was not the case.

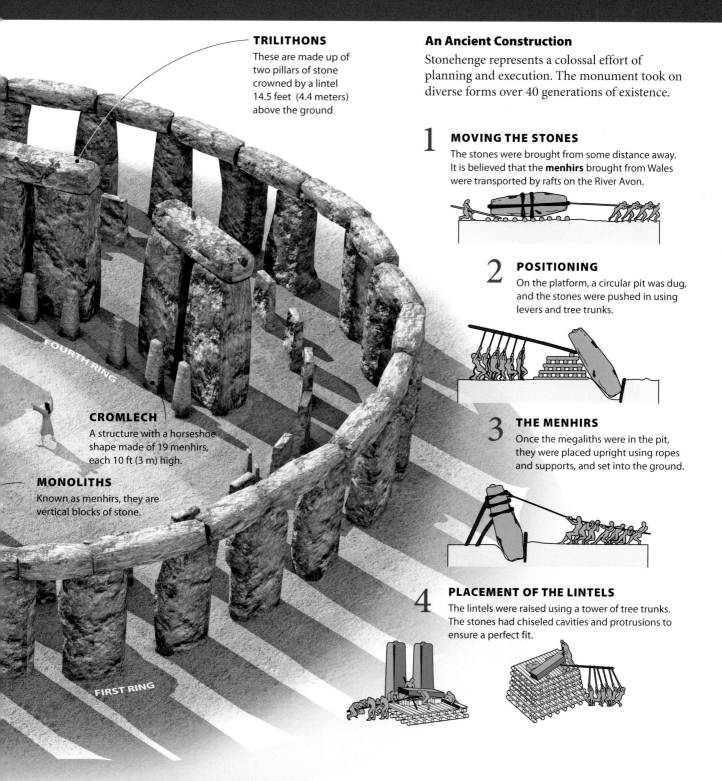

TRILITHONS
These are made up of two pillars of stone crowned by a lintel 14.5 feet (4.4 meters) above the ground

FOURTH RING

CROMLECH
A structure with a horseshoe shape made of 19 menhirs, each 10 ft (3 m) high.

MONOLITHS
Known as menhirs, they are vertical blocks of stone.

FIRST RING

An Ancient Construction

Stonehenge represents a colossal effort of planning and execution. The monument took on diverse forms over 40 generations of existence.

1 MOVING THE STONES
The stones were brought from some distance away. It is believed that the **menhirs** brought from Wales were transported by rafts on the River Avon.

2 POSITIONING
On the platform, a circular pit was dug, and the stones were pushed in using levers and tree trunks.

3 THE MENHIRS
Once the megaliths were in the pit, they were placed upright using ropes and supports, and set into the ground.

4 PLACEMENT OF THE LINTELS
The lintels were raised using a tower of tree trunks. The stones had chiseled cavities and protrusions to ensure a perfect fit.

Prehistoric Building

The **megalithic** structure of Stonehenge was built on Salisbury Plain, in the south of England. Its design combines stone, wood, and earth. It was built over a period of more than 1,400 years and, according to **archaeologists,** it is one of the most important **prehistoric** constructions in Europe.

The Evolution of Prehistoric Architecture

The megalithic ruins are located some 80 miles (130 kilometers) west of London. While it is unclear today exactly why they were built, we are certain they were used to mark astronomical events and as a burial sanctuary.

GREAT CURSUS

2 miles (3.2 kilometers) of channeled road was built around 3500 B.C. Its purpose is unknown.

STONEHENGE

After the Great Cursus, a construction technique was developed that converted Stonehenge into one of the most architecturally advanced works of the time and place.

THE AVENUE

The journey that symbolized the passing from life to death continued on the cobbled avenue after coming down the River Avon from Durrington Walls.

① **2950-2900 B.C.**

In the middle of the **Neolithic** Age, the embankment was prepared and the circular trench was dug. Directly inside the earthen bank is what is known as the "Aubrey Circle."

LEGEND

■ Settlement, 2600-2400 B.C.

● Stone Age monuments

⋯ Avenue

— Present day roads

River Avon

A 3085

SALISBURY PLAIN

LAND OF THE LIVING

A 3028

Durrington Walls ■ South Circle ●

Cuckoo Stone ● ●

Great Cursus

Woodhenge

A 3028

Enlarged area

A 3086

A 360

A 344

A 303

Stonehenge ●

A 303

Bluehenge ●

LAND OF THE ANCESTORS

WILTSHIRE

A 360

River Avon

A 345

N

0   miles   3

UNITED KINGDOM — Enlarged area

Stonehenge □ ● London

Enlarged area

Could It Have Been a Place of Healing?

Astronomical observatory, religious temple ... There is no shortage of theories to explain the origin of Stonehenge. In 2008, British archaeologist Tim Darvill risked yet another: After finding various bones with different injuries during an excavation sponsored by the British Broadcasting Corporation (BBC), Darvill suggested that Stonehenge could have been a place to which pilgrims traveled to cure their sicknesses and injuries.

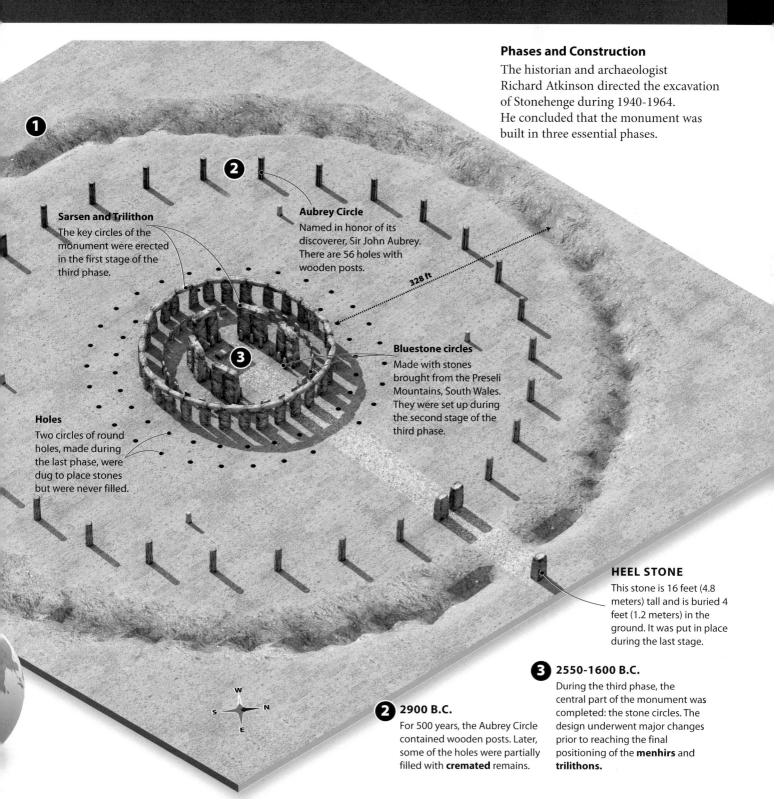

Phases and Construction

The historian and archaeologist Richard Atkinson directed the excavation of Stonehenge during 1940-1964. He concluded that the monument was built in three essential phases.

Sarsen and Trilithon
The key circles of the monument were erected in the first stage of the third phase.

Aubrey Circle
Named in honor of its discoverer, Sir John Aubrey. There are 56 holes with wooden posts.

328 ft

Bluestone circles
Made with stones brought from the Preseli Mountains, South Wales. They were set up during the second stage of the third phase.

Holes
Two circles of round holes, made during the last phase, were dug to place stones but were never filled.

HEEL STONE
This stone is 16 feet (4.8 meters) tall and is buried 4 feet (1.2 meters) in the ground. It was put in place during the last stage.

3 2550-1600 B.C.
During the third phase, the central part of the monument was completed: the stone circles. The design underwent major changes prior to reaching the final positioning of the **menhirs** and **trilithons.**

2 2900 B.C.
For 500 years, the Aubrey Circle contained wooden posts. Later, some of the holes were partially filled with **cremated** remains.

1,000 Years of Work

Recent studies have shown that the construction of Stonehenge required about 1,000 years of work from large numbers of people. According to the most convincing theory thus far, they were built in connection with the development of religious rites and astronomical observation, to which the priests of the people were devoted.

The Heel Stone

The circle is the dominant site at Stonehenge. The northeast side of the circle opens up into a wide pathway, which at some point appears to have been the main entrance to the **henge.** And at the opposite side from the pathway, and outside of the circle, a solitary **monolith** was put up. It was named the Heel Stone because of its shape.

TECHNIQUE The arches and circular shapes at Stonehenge show the builders' advanced mastery of geometry.

How Did the Stones Get to Stonehenge?

While Stonehenge is mostly associated with the **sandstone monoliths** that were expertly carved to support **lintels** of the same size, the smaller blocks, called **bluestones,** are the most mysterious.

The chemical analysis of the almost 80 bluestones found today at Stonehenge revealed that they came from the Preseli Hills, situated in southeast Wales. The tests were so precise that it was possible to locate their origin in an area called Carn Menyn. They were slabs of dark-colored and finely textured volcanic rocks. These stones form great peaks, and they were probably beloved by the people of the era. These rocks are white or cream in color, but they are called "bluestones" because they look blue when they become wet with rain.

Thanks to the natural shape of these peaks, the designers of Stonehenge only had to chip away at the stones from the base to separate them from the rock face. The most common question, of course, is—how did they transport them?

The most logical route, of around 249 miles (400 kilometers), would have included moving several dozen blocks of around 4 tons (3.6 metric tons) each, using wooden platforms rolled over greased guides, to the waters of the East Cleddau River. Rafts made out of tree trunks would then have been used to navigate the Daugleddau estuary, the Atlantic coast of the Bristol channel, and the River Avon, near Avon county (not the same river as the one near Stonehenge, though it has the same name). Then, the ancient Britons would have had to travel by land again to arrive at Stonehenge.

They completed the entire route dragging the heavy blocks and using only human power. We know this because in England in 2500 B.C., pack animals had not yet been domesticated.

A COMPLICATED ROUTE

The difficult route also required some level of diplomacy: The workers had to cross the lands of other clans. They also would have needed a good sense of direction and a detailed knowledge of the geography of the area because the route involved constant changes of direction and included various smaller journeys between nearby waterways. It is not known whether these nearly 80 blocks were carried during one trip. This strategy would have involved hundreds of young and able-bodied men leaving their homes, crops, cattle, and hunting. Additionally, they may have had to leave their clans defenseless to take part in the venture. This leads to the theory that the bluestone blocks were hauled to the site over a period of several years.

Bluehenge, the Last Great Enigma

One of the most recent and interesting discoveries near Stonehenge is another **henge** 82 feet (25 meters) in diameter, which held a stone circle and was located at the point where Stonehenge's Avenue reached the River Avon, 1 mile (1.6 kilometers) to the southwest of the burial monument.

This newly found circle revealed a significant fact: The remains of bluestones were found inside it, like those brought from the Preseli Hills to build Stonehenge. For this reason, **archaeologists** named it Bluehenge (some call it Bluestonehenge).

Experts suspect that around 25 of the bluestones that ended up at Stonehenge were previously in this circle, based on a series of holes that were also found at this site.

Later research additionally suggested that Bluehenge could have been the site where bodies were **cremated** after being transported downriver from Durrington Walls village and before being buried at Stonehenge.

THE BLUESTONES at Stonehenge were quarried from the Preseli Hills in southeast Wales (left).

How Was the Stonehenge Complex Built?

The builders of Stonehenge employed original and advanced methods for their time in **Neolithic** Europe.

Nearly all of the stone circles at Stonehenge are made of unpolished **monoliths.** The **bluestones** used in the first phases of Stonehenge's construction were put in place there just as they were quarried from the ground. The exceptions to this rule are the **sarsens.** The monoliths from the last phases of construction were carefully smoothed down to an oblong shape that is better for forming part of a much more complex construction. Effectively, the builders of the final phase of Stonehenge took a huge leap forward in the design of this type of monument when they designed structures with **lintels.** While the latest research suggests that the bluestone circle could have

also been covered by lintels, this theory has not been tested and no evidence of this possibility remains. Half of Stonehenge's linteled structures made out of sarsens have lasted 4,500 years, which highlights the great ability of this last generation of builders during the transition between the Neolithic Period and the British **Bronze Age.** Silica **sandstone** is a **sedimentary** rock widely used in construction. It is possible to shape it with tools made of the same stone. However, this is a difficult task because the stone splits into tiny pieces. Study of the monoliths indicates that various people worked individual surfaces.

SURPRISING TECHNIQUES

Although the construction did not reach the level of per-

fection of walls built in later periods, the blocks of sandstone at Stonehenge come reasonably close to that which a Roman or medieval (from A.D. 400-1400) stonemason might call an *ashlar.* (An ashlar is a stone carved into the shape of a brick.) The monoliths that are vertically positioned also use a technique employed by the ancient Greeks in their temple columns. This technique involves a widening in the middle area of the column to correct the visual illusion that a straight shaft looks concave. But the most surprising thing about the Stonehenge construction is the use of the dovetail technique that allowed the blocks to be placed without using mortar: The lintels fit into each other and to the monoliths that support them.

RECONSTRUCTION
A group of archaeologists in Gloucestershire, a county in England, reproduce the mechanisms for moving such monoliths as those at Stonehenge.

FUNCTIONAL CARVING
The stones were carved into matching bumps and cavities to make a perfect joint between columns and lintels.

How Did They Raise the Stones?

A recent experiment demonstrated that a group of approximately 150 people can lift a monolith of a weight and size similar to the largest of those at Stonehenge (some 27 tons, or 25 metric tons). Scholars today think this is approximately the number of people who worked on raising a stone in the circle.

In the 1940's, British **archaeologist** Richard Atkinson worked out that Stonehenge's construction occurred over centuries in three phases.

The first was between 2950 and 2900 B.C., when the ancient Britons made the **embankment** and the circular trench; the next in 2900 B.C., when they erected some 80 blocks of bluestone, arranged in the shape of a horseshoe; and the last between 2550 and 1600 B.C., when the bluestones were moved into their current positions on the inside of the circle. This was also when they moved the Slaughter Stone (see page 25) opposite the **trilithons** brought from the south of Wales. According to Atkinson, Stonehenge was abandoned around 1500 B.C. and left in a similar condition to that in which it is found today.

Given the length of time over which Stonehenge was built, it makes sense that different methods may have been used at different times and that the ancient Britons learned as they went on how best to shift and raise the stones.

What Was the Purpose of Stonehenge?

Why was Stonehenge really built? In recent years a good number of long-held theories about Stonehenge have been rejected. Its real purpose remains elusive.

In England, generation after generation of natives have asked themselves to what purpose were the stones lying in a circle in the plains of Salisbury placed. During more than 30 centuries (Stonehenge was abandoned in around 1500 B.C.) the people of England, as well as foreign visitors, have come up with theories, some far-fetched and others based on the historical and **archaeological** knowledge of the time.

During the Middle Ages, the monument was linked with the magical activities of Merlin, the Welsh magician to the legendary King Arthur. At this time, people believed that the stones came from Ireland.

Later, early attempts to make the study of Stonehenge more scientific came into conflict with supersti-tious traditions. In the 1600's, people still said that anyone who tried to count the stones of the monument would die.

In the 1700's, William Stukeley, a physician, clergyman, and *antiquarian* (a person who studies or collects relics from ancient times), contributed some of the first archaeological findings about the stone circle. Fascinated by the **Druids,** Stukeley mistaken-ly attributed Stonehenge to this learned, priestly class among the **Celts,** an ancient people of Europe. He was also the first to recognize the alignment of Stonehenge with the **sol-stices.** Stukeley proposed that Stonehenge was completed in 460 B.C., which we now know was off by about 2,500 years. His theories were important to the study of Stonehenge because his was the first attempt to associate the alignment of Stonehenge with the seasons.

A TEMPLE DEDICATED TO THE SUN

Stukeley's demonstration that Stonehenge was aligned with the sunrise on the summer solstice led subsequent archaeologists, both professional and ama-teur, to suggest two major theories: that the monu-ment was a temple dedicat-ed to the sun; or an obser-vatory establishing an annual calendar.

Modern archaeologists have chosen to distance themselves from these the-ories. The nearby remains of Woodhenge and Durrington Walls, as well as the sites where the stone blocks for the monument were extracted, have become the principal field

A Bluestone Altar

The outer ring of Stonehenge is made up of vertical oblong stones of **sandstone** crowned by **lintels**. Inside this outer ring, another circle is found, made up of smaller **bluestone,** which encircles another structure in a horseshoe shape, also built of sandstone rocks. Inside it is the slab known as the Slaughter Stone.

What Was the Significance of the Bluestones?

One of the great mysteries that surrounds Stonehenge is that of the bluestones with which the first circle of stones was made around 2500 B.C. The latest theories suggest that the Preseli Hills in Wales, and in particular the location of Carn Menyn, the exact source of the bluestone, were places of worship. Cuts in the rocks of the region have been found, dating back to the **Neolithic** Period. In this sense, the second stage of Stonehenge would have artificially reproduced the great scenery of Carn Menyn.

To what end? Perhaps simply as a demonstration of the power of the local rulers—capable of bringing part of the sanctuary to their jurisdiction—or to transfer the supposed healing power of these stones to Stonehenge. The belief that the natural springs of the Preseli Hills have healing qualities, which was widespread in the area until recent times, supports this latter theory.

of research to discover the function of Stonehenge.

A VAST CEMETERY

A new theory centers on the human remains buried around the monument. The dating of these remains shows that Stonehenge had a definite burial purpose since its creation around the year 3000 B.C., until after the construction of the ring of **sandstones**, some 500 years later.

According to Mike Parker Pearson, professor of **archaeology** and co-director of the Stonehenge Riverside Project, the monument was erected to honor ancestors. Drawing on his

knowledge of the *indigenous* (native) cultures of Madagascar, Parker Pearson arrived at the conclusion that the stones could symbolize the stiffening of the body after death as well as represent the everlastingness of eternal life; while the wooden constructions, made from less permanent material, could represent the brief earthly life. Although the high number of burials discovered—240 total—make Stonehenge the largest **Neolithic** cemetery in England, the long period over which these ceremonies were celebrated makes experts think that only members of a ruling tribal family were buried at the mon-

ument. This fact leads experts to suppose that the neighboring henges of Durrington Walls and Woodhenge were considered the land of the living, in contrast to Stonehenge, the land of the dead.

The fact that both places appear to be connected to the river by avenues gives rise to the idea of a ceremonial circuit that represents the transition, or shift, from life to death.

According to Parker Pearson's theory, the bodies of the members of the ruling family were taken from Durrington Walls to the river. They were then floated down the river several miles on rafts made of tree

trunks; then carried to the avenue and on to Stonehenge, where the remains were buried after **cremation.** According to Parker Pearson's theory, the remains of ordinary people of the region were not found because they were cremated and their ashes thrown into the river.

Other recent theories suggest that Stonehenge was a multifunctional center—cemetery, astronomical observatory, solar temple, and healing sanctuary. This possibility would reconcile two of the known facts about the monument: that it is filled with cremated human remains and that it is oriented toward the first sunrise of summer.

The Mysterious *"Cursus"*

The furrowed road, which is 2 miles (3.2 kilometers) long and 479 feet (146 meters) wide, was built 500 years before the first Stonehenge. Oriented toward the daybreak on the **equinoxes** in spring and autumn, it was called "cursus" by an antique dealer, William Stukeley, who wrongly believed it was the remains of a chariot race stadium built by the Romans.

Astronomical Calendars

Cultures around the world created **astronomical calendars** during the **Neolithic** Period.

The Rise of Agriculture

Around the world, people of many Neolithic cultures created astronomical calendars—calendars that make use of sunlight entering a certain gate or window on a certain day—to mark special times for religious celebration or to follow the seasons. These calendars developed independently. One thing that marks Neolithic culture is the rise of agriculture. As a people without writing began to practice agriculture and need to follow the seasons, this means of marking time evolved in many places.

EGYPT—NABTA PLAYA

This site (above) in the Sahara Desert is a reconstruction based on **archaeological** evidence of a stone circle built by the shore of a small seasonal lake around 6000 B.C. At the site, large **sandstone** blocks, weighing several tons each, were lined up with the four *cardinal directions* (north, east, south, and west) and the sun.

GERMANY—GOSECK CIRCLE

This site (left) in central Germany is a reconstruction of the wooden **henge** that existed here around 4900 B.C. Archaeologists used holes still left in the ground to show where the new posts should be placed. The Goseck Circle contains two gates in its wooden rings that align with sunrise and sunset on the days of the summer and winter **solstice.**

SUNRISE AT NEWGRANGE ON THE SOLSTICE

Light floods the passage at Newgrange for about 17 minutes during the morning of the winter solstice. Today, light fills the chamber about 4.5 minutes after sunrise. Astronomers have calculated, however, that 5,000 years ago the chamber would have filled with sunlight at the moment of sunrise.

IRELAND—NEWGRANGE

The Irish burial site Newgrange was built around 3200 B.C. Inside this huge mound are passageways. On one day a year—the sunrise of the winter solstice—the sun floods a passageway inside (see inset above).

The Tombs of Amesbury

A **funerary** (burial) site containing the remains of two men was discovered in Amesbury, near Stonehenge, in 2002. One of the bodies is called the "Amesbury Archer," because of the arrowheads found in his grave. **Archaeologists** date the tombs at Amesbury to about 2300 B.C., around the time that the first stones at Stonehenge were raised. The men were found with more than 100 objects, from arrowheads and copper knives, to gold pendants.

Dating Objects from the Past

Carbon atoms *decay* (break down by releasing particles) at an exact and uniform rate. This allows scientists to determine the age of objects by measuring the amount of carbon-14 in an item. A broad range of information can be determined through dating archaeological remains: how much food and other resources ancient peoples used, the range over which they traveled, and the characteristics of the environment they lived in, among other things.

Carbon-14 dating studies performed on archaeological pieces from Stonehenge some years ago at Oxford University showed that the most likely date for the raising of the first stones was the year 2300 B.C.

KNIVES
Copper knives, with well-sharpened points and of different sizes were discovered in the graves. Knives made of gold were also found.

BLACK STONE
Called a "cushion stone" because of its similarity to the cushions of a sofa, this stone was used as an anvil to work metal. Gold and copper were new to the people of the period in which Stonehenge was raised, and they had to seek out elements to work them.

CARBON-14
During the excavation headed by British archaeologist Tim Darvill, 100 pieces of organic material from the bases of the original sandstone blocks were uncovered. Fourteen were selected for analysis using carbon-14 dating.

TUSK
It is thought that these tusks belonged to a wild boar or an animal of similar size, and that they were used as ornaments.

Prehistoric Migration

Analysis of the molars and premolars of the two adults found in the Amesbury tombs revealed that these people were in one place until six years of age and in another until age thirteen (possibly in the northwestern portion of Britain, Wales, or Brittany). "This is the best example of prehistoric migration in Europe found to this day," stated British archaeologist Andrew Fitzpatrick.

EARRINGS

Made of gold, the earrings represent the earliest samples of jewelry work from the period. They were found in pairs.

ARMBANDS

Used as protection during hunting, the armbands also appeared to be a status symbol in the **Celtic** community. They were made of polished stone.

ORIGIN

Archaeologists claim that the "Amesbury Archer" came from the Alps near Switzerland and Germany. Had he relocated to Stonehenge? Was he only visiting the site to be healed of an illness? The archer was approximately 40 at the time of his death. The other man was 20. Because of an unusual genetic trait, scientists know the two men were related.

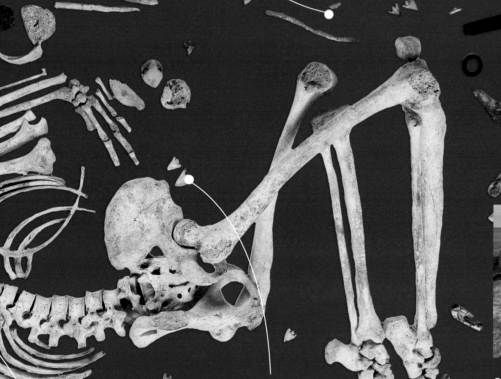

ARROWHEADS

Fifteen arrowheads were found near the body of the "Amesbury Archer."

OTHER TOMBS

A year after the discovery of the tomb of the archer and his companion, and less than half a mile (0.8 kilometer) away, other tombs from the same period containing the remains of seven people were found, four of them men.

What Was Life Like in the Time of the Archer?

Until 4000 B.C., the tribes that populated England were **nomadic** (they moved from place to place as a way of obtaining food). These nomads lived by hunting, gathering, and fishing. In the **Neolithic** Period, they abandoned this simpler life and began raising grains and livestock.

When construction of Stonehenge began, around 3000 B.C., the people of southwest England lived in very small groups. They did, however, sometimes gather in larger communities to complete more difficult tasks, such as the construction of a henge.

Archaeologists have calculated that the third phase of construction on Stonehenge required 2 million hours of work, the equivalent of 2 years of labor for 300 people working 10 hours a day. How-ever, it is likely that the various clans in the region only dedicated part of the year to Stonehenge's construction, prolonging the task. The most recent research has calculated that in the settlement of Durrington Walls,

near Stonehenge, there were 1,000 dwellings. The size of this village reinforces the theory that this settlement was raised to house the monument's builders and visitors arriving from various points in the region. In addition, analysis of the remains suggests that stays at Durrington Walls were temporary. People appeared to have moved into the settlement to help with the monument's construction, bringing what was needed to stay for a few months at a time.

NOMADISM AS THE NORM
Although they were largely stationary, Neolithic Britons also maintained nomadic habits to some extent. It was not unusual for them to spend part of the year away from their original region. Every 10 to

20 years, they were essentially forced to leave the area where they lived and move in search of new ground to farm; they did not yet know the farming techniques necessary to protect the soil's nutrients.

This factor, combined with the destructive effects of ever-larger herds of cattle and goats, caused the region to lose a good part of its dense birch and pine forests in only a few centuries. As a result, meadows were already the dominant landscape by the time work began on Stonehenge.

By the time of the Archer's lifetime—about 2300 B.C.—the people of ancient England had made a complete shift from a nomadic lifestyle of hunting to one of farming. And, they had developed the technical abilities to build the final phase of Stonehenge.

The Case of the "Amesbury Archer"

A group of archaeologists found two **prehistoric** tombs near Amesbury, a little more than 2 miles (3.2 kilometers) from Stonehenge. The older man's tomb contained the best prehistoric **funerary** offerings found in England, including gold jewelry (the oldest remains of this type found on the islands); arrowheads; copper knives; and pieces of bell-shaped ceramics—a pottery technique commonly found on the continent throughout the period, but not in England. Analysis of dental remains turned up surprising information: The "Amesbury Archer" (the older man) was not a native of England, but of the Swiss Alps. His young relative, however, had been born locally.

Durrington Walls, a Camp for Workers?

Recent **archaeological** work at the Durrington Walls site, which contains two circles (northern and southern), and nearby Woodhenge formed the basis of a convincing theory regarding Stonehenge's purpose.

I n 1812, a large **henge** was discovered near the small town of Durrington, 2 miles (3.2 kilometers) northeast of Stonehenge, in a bend of the Bristol River Avon. The circle was enormous, measuring 1,500 feet (457.2 meters) in diameter, equivalent to 20 times the size of Stonehenge. Despite its closeness to the **megalithic** monument, the site was not excavated for the first time until 1966. At the start of the 2000's, it still kept nearly all of its secrets. Finally, in 2003, the henge of Durrington Walls, which is crossed by a regional high-way, became the central focus of the Stonehenge Riverside Project.

The project leaders discovered seven **Neolithic** dwellings to the east of the circle. These dwellings were built between 2600 and 2500 B.C., during the same period in which the **bluestones** were placed at Stonehenge. Researchers concluded that there may have been more than a thousand dwellings like those found, a figure that makes Durrington Walls the largest Neolithic settlement known in Britain. In one of the houses, archaeologists found signs of primitive wooden furniture and ceramic remnants, as well as animal bones, clear indications that the people of this area slept and ate here, at least during part of the year, suggesting it may have housed seasonal workers.

VARIOUS RITUALS

Researchers also noted the scarcity of human remains, deducing that the population typically burned the bodies of their people and spread their ashes in the river. The remains of their leaders, however, appear to have been carried to Stonehenge in a ritual **procession** and *interred* (buried) near the great rock monument.

Seahenge: Preserved Wood

To understand the nature of henges with wood circles, archaeologists had to travel to a small coastal town in the eastern part of the United Kingdom, Holme-next-the-Sea. Near this village, in 1998 the best-preserved prehistoric wooden henge was found: Seahenge (right), comprised of 55 tree trunks forming a circle some 23 feet (7 meters) in diameter, preserved by mud. In the center of the circle, the remains of an enormous inverted oak, with its roots for branches, was found. Scientists learned that the henge, whose magnificent state of preservation has been very useful in studying these wooden monuments, was constructed in 2049 B.C., during the transition between the Neolithic Period and the **Bronze Age.**

SEASONAL POPULATION
The broad circle of Durrington Walls, where dwellings of wood were built and lived in by the builders of Stonehenge.

Durrington Walls House

Archaeological studies show that the houses that made up the village are 4,600 years old. According to these studies, the village was a seasonal settlement housing people who traveled there with prepared foods and animals and stayed only at certain times of the year.

A Village of Builders

According to studies done by the British archaeologist Mike Parker Pearson, the Durrington Walls area consisted of an extensive circular village with more than 300 houses. With such dimensions, it was without a doubt one of the biggest villages in northwestern Europe. "We believe both men and women, and even children, lived there. And it would not have been unusual for all of them to have participated in the construction of the Stonehenge complex," noted Parker Pearson.

Stone Age Remains

In one of the well-preserved houses found during excavations by the National Geographic Society, researchers found objects from daily life during the **Stone Age:** flint tools (axes, for example), the point of a brooch (brohch—an ornamental pin) from a dress, and two small recesses in the corners of the house.

HOUSES OF CLAY, MORTAR, AND REEDS

After excavation work carried out in 2007, archaeologists found houses that in some cases had walls made of a mixture of ground clay and mortar (cobb), and in other cases had walls of reeds covered with mortar.

THE KITCHEN

In the center of the house, archaeologists found remnants of an oval stove and two gutters with ash stains around them. "Whoever cooked there was definitely kneeling," maintained Mike Parker Pearson.

Stonehenge's Treasures

From 2003 to 2009, the Stonehenge Riverside Project was headed by **archaeologist** Mike Parker Pearson, then with the University of Sheffield. The project uncovered details about the life of the community that built the magnificent monument, thanks to the items found in various excavations in the area.

Dwelling Foundations

A decade ago, a group of archaeologists under Mike Parker Pearson found foundations for dwellings (right) dating back to the period in which construction on Stonehenge began. Excavations in the area surrounding the **megalithic** monument revealed the remains of eight wooden buildings, and study of the surrounding areas has revealed up to 30 additional dwellings. A group of smaller dwellings was also found under the **embankment**.

According to Parker Pearson, the cracks appearing in the plaster floor indicate that the local inhabitants cooked there. The remains of furnishings were also found in five of the dwellings. Test excavations and geophysical surveying have detected a multitude of additional possible chimneys in the valley. "I believe that we may find up to 300 dwellings at this site," Parker Pearson said during the excavation. If this is true, that makes it the largest **Neolithic** settlement found in Britain to date.

CONTAINER FOR BURNING INCENSE

GNEISS STONE

This perforated and curiously polished stone is made of gneiss, a metamorphic rock composed of the same minerals

found in granite (quartz, feldspar, and mica), which was heavily used by the Britons who built Stonehenge

Horns and Bones of Livestock

According to studies by specialists, the workers who built Stonehenge managed to make precise holes in the ground using meager digging tools made of the horns and bones of livestock. Archaeologists found these items buried in the deepest area of "the ditch," as it is referred to in English literature.

AXE

The axe head is made of silex or flint, a material used frequently during the **Stone Age.** Its durability is ideal for making cutting tools.

Arrowheads

Like the axes and other tools used by the Britons, the arrowheads found in the excavations were made of stone found in the Cornwall area, on the shores of the **Celtic** Sea.

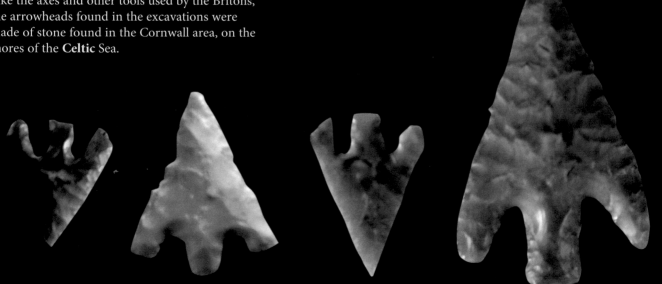

RING OF BRODGAR

This **henge** is part of the Heart of **Neolithic** Orkney, in the Orkney Islands. It forms part of a complex dating from the same era as Stonehenge.

Places to See and Visit

OTHER PLACES OF INTEREST

AVEBURY
UNITED KINGDOM

A few miles from Stonehenge, this pretty and well-preserved town has a major attraction for those interested in **archaeological** treasures: the Avebury Ring, a ring of stones that dates to the same period as Stonehenge.

BLUEHENGE
UNITED KINGDOM

Some years ago, a group of scientists discovered evidence of what they called "a second Stonehenge," with characteristics similar to the original. This archaeological site is located a little over 1 mile (1.6 kilometers) from the famous monument and was named "Bluehenge" by M. Parker Pearson and specialists from the University of Sheffield. Excavations show that a stone circle 30 feet (9 meters) in diameter was erected here, a complex that may have been surrounded by a ditch many years ago. It is also thought that the gigantic chunks of **bluestone** were brought from the Preseli Hills, more than 150 miles (241 kilometers) away.

Stonehenge

MEGALITHIC MONUMENT

Normal visiting hours at Stonehenge are from 9 am to 7 pm, depending on weather conditions, which are generally less favorable in winter.

DURRINGTON WALLS

The excavations performed at this site, 2 miles (3.2 kilometers) north of Stonehenge, indicate that it is the largest human settlement from the **Neolithic** Period in Britain, eventually housing a community of several thousand inhabitants. It is surrounded by an enormous **henge** some 1,500 feet (457 meters) in diameter. Despite the discovery of the remains of dwellings and utensils there, most of its secrets remain unknown.

THE AVENUE

This **processional** road cuts through the ditch surrounding Stonehenge. Known as "The Avenue," this paved road aligns with the summer **solstice.** It was discovered in the 1600's, and it connects Stonehenge to the River Avon.

Heel Stone

This stone can be seen from Stonehenge. During the summer solstice, on around June 21, the sun peeks over the top of this stone, which has led to theories about its astronomical function.

CHICHÉN ITZÁ
MEXICO

The site may look very different, but a number of buildings at Chichén Itzá were used as calendars for astronomical events. El Caracol aligns with the solstices and El Castillo marks the **equinox.**

CAHOKIA
UNITED STATES

A reconstructed wood circle that was used as an astronomical calendar by native Americans can be seen in Illinois at Cahokia, the site of one of the largest **prehistoric** communities in the Americas. Archaeologists estimate that 10,000 to 20,000 people may have lived at Cahokia at its peak, between A.D. 1050 and 1150.

Glossary

Archaeology—The scientific study of the remains of past human cultures.

Astronomical calendar—A calendar made by positioning wooden posts or stone columns in the correct places in a circle. The sun would mark the day of an important astronomical event by shining through a certain opening or gate.

Bluestone—Dark, volcanic stone.

Bronze Age—The period when people began to use bronze, an alloy (mixture) of copper and tin, for tools and weapons. The Bronze Age is the second age of a three-age classification system originally developed to describe the prehistory of Europe. In this system, the Bronze Age followed the Stone Age and came before the Iron Age.

Celts — A culture of tribal people who lived in Europe during the Iron Age.

Cremate—To burn a dead body to ash.

Concentric circles—Differently sized circles centered on one point.

Cromlech—A circle of large stones erected by prehistoric people.

Druid—A learned, priestly class among the Celts of ancient France, Britain, and Ireland. We know almost nothing about the religion they practiced. They were likely active between 200 B.C. and A.D. 200 to 400.

Eclipse — The darkening of a planet or moon. It occurs when the shadow of one object in space falls on another object or when one object moves in front of another to block its light.

Embankment—A raised bank of earth or stones.

Equinox — Either of the two moments each year when the sun is directly above Earth's equator.

Funerary—Having to do with burial.

Henge—A stone- or wood-circle complex of prehistoric origin made up of a circular embankment with smaller circular areas in the middle.

Lintel—A horizontal stone placed on top of two stone columns.

Megalith—Structures made of large stones by prehistoric people.

Menhir—A large vertical stone erected as part of a stone circle.

Monolith—A column made of a single large stone.

Neolithic—Of the later Stone Age, marked by the beginning of farming and raising animals, and the use of polished stone weapons and tools.

Nomadic—Moving from place to place as a way of obtaining food.

Prehistoric—Events that occurred before the invention of writing.

Procession—Ceremonial parade.

Sandstone—A type of rock made up chiefly of sand that has been "cemented" together by pressure or minerals.

Sarsen—Sandstone blocks.

Sedimentary — Rock formed when mineral matter or remains of plants and animals (sediment) settle out of water or, less commonly, out of air or ice

Solstice — One of the two moments each year when the sun is at either its northernmost or southernmost position. In the Northern Hemisphere, the sun is at its southernmost point at the winter solstice—around December 21—the shortest period of day of the year. In that hemisphere, the sun is at its northernmost on around June 21—the summer solstice—the longest day of the year.

Stone Age—A period in the development of humans that lasted from around 2.5 million years ago until individual cultures began using metal tools instead of stone tools. The date varies based on when that development occurred in a culture. In some areas of the Middle East and Asia, metal tools have been dated from as early as 8,000 years ago, while in Europe the Stone Age ended around 6,000 years ago.

Trilithons—Two stones standing upright with a stone across the top.

For Further Information

Books

Aronson, Marc, and Michael Parker Pearson. *If Stones Could Speak: Unlocking the Secrets of Stonehenge.* Washington, D.C.: National Geographic, 2010. Print.

Chippindale, Christopher. *Stonehenge Complete.* 4th ed. New York: Thames & Hudson, 2012. Print.

Gray, Leon. *Solving the Mysteries of Stonehenge.* New York: Marshall Cavendish, 2009. Print.

Henzel, Cynthia Kennedy. *Stonehenge.* Edina, MN: ABDO Pub., 2011. Print.

Richards, Julian. *Stonehenge.* 3rd ed. London: English Heritage, 2013. Print.

Websites

Alexander, Caroline. "Stonehenge." *National Geographic.* National Geographic Society, June 2008. Web. 06 Mar. 2014.

"Art of Stonehenge." *Salisbury & South Wiltshire Museum.* Salisbury & South Wiltshire Museum, n.d. Web. 06 Mar. 2014.

"Discover Stonehenge." *English Heritage.* English Heritage, n.d. Web. 03 Mar. 2014.

Jones, Dan. "New Light on Stonehenge." *Smithsonian.com.* Smithsonian, Oct. 2008. Web. 06 Mar. 2014.

"Stonehenge, Avebury and Associated Sites." *UNESCO World Heritage Centre.* UNESCO, 2014. Web. 05 Mar. 2014.

Index

Acknowledgments

Pictures:

© Adam Stanford, Aerial Cam (www.aerial-cam.co.uk)

© AGE Fotostock

© Alamy Images

AP Photo

© BoyneValleyTours (www.boynevalleytours.com)

© Corbis Images

© Crown copyright/NMR

Images Courtesy of Archives and Special Collections, Dickinson College, Carlisle, PA

© English Heritage/NMR © Getty Images

© Lynette Thomas, The Image File

© National Geographic Stock

© Science Photo Library

© Thinkstock

© Wessex Archaeology (www.wessexarch.co.uk)

© Wiltshire Heritage Museum/Devizes